Time

Thea Fel [...]

KINGFISHER

First published 2014 by Kingfisher
an imprint of Macmillan Children's Books
20 New Wharf Road, London N1 9RR
Associated companies throughout the world
www.panmacmillan.com

Series editor: Polly Goodman
Literacy consultant: Ellie Costa, Bank Street School for Children, New York
UK literacy consultant: Hilary Horton

ISBN: 978-0-7534-3665-3

Copyright © Macmillan Publishers International Ltd 2014

9 8 7 6 5 4
4TR/0318/WKT/UG/105MA

A CIP catalogue record for this book is available from the British Library.

Printed in China

Picture credits
The Publisher would like to thank the following for permission to reproduce their material.
Top = t; Bottom = b; Centre = c; Left = l; Right = r
Cover Shutterstock / Samuel Borges Photography, 3 Alamy/Andrew Holt, 4 Shutterstock/
wavebreakmedia, 5 Shutterstock/Adrian Niederhaeuser, 6t Shutterstock/poonsap, 6b Shutterstock/
Tatyana Vychegzhanina, 7t Shutterstock/Monkey Business Images, 7b Shutterstock/Bienchen-s,
8–9 Shutterstock/Morgan Lane Photography, 9t Corbis/Juice Images, 10 Shutterstock/Adrian
Niederhaeuser, 11 Shutterstock/oriontrail, 12 Shutterstock/Monkey Business Images, 13t Nutshell
Media/Howard Davies, 13b Kingfisher Artbank/Michael Wicks, 14–15 Shutterstock/Simon Bratt,
16t Shutterstock/Noam Armonn, 16–17 Alamy/Juice Images, 18 Shutterstock/Kotomiti Okuma,
19 Alamy/Purestock, 20 Shutterstock/Simon Bratt, 21 Shutterstock/Adrian Niederhaeuser,
22 Shutterstock/Herbert Kratky, 23 Shutterstock/Olga Sapegina, 24 Shutterstock/Yurlick,
25t Shutterstock/Monkey Business Images, 25b Nutshell Media/Howard Davies, 26 Shutterstock/
Ho Yeow Hui, 27 Shutterstock/3445128471, 28–29 Corbis/Ocean, 30–31 Shutterstock/Elena Efimova.

The sun rises.

It is morning.

You wake up
in the morning.

Good morning!

What time is it?

The small hand is on seven.

The big hand is on twelve.

It is seven o'clock.

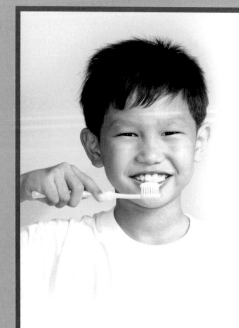

In the morning, you brush your teeth.

You wash your face.

You get dressed.

You eat breakfast.

Most children go to school
in the morning.

Most grown-ups
go to work
in the morning.

The morning ends at noon.

Both hands of the clock are on twelve.

This time is also called midday.

At noon, the sun is high
in the sky.

Many people eat lunch at noon

After noon, it is the afternoon!

You finish school in the afternoon.

After school, you can do many things.

The afternoon ends
when the sun sets.

Now it is evening.

In the evening your family makes dinner.

Then you get to eat it!

Evening becomes night.

You brush your teeth
and wash your face.

Now you are ready
for a bedtime story!

While you are asleep, the day ends and a new one begins.

This happens at **midnight**.

At midnight, it is very dark outside.

Both hands of the clock are on twelve.

One day is 24 hours long.

One **hour** is 60 minutes long.

An American football game is 60 minutes long.

One minute is 60 seconds long.

A **second** is as fast as a clap of your hands.

There are seven days in one **week**.

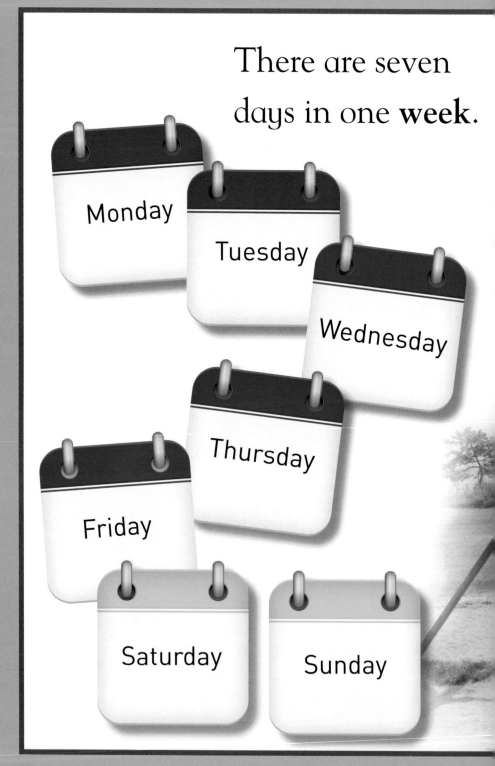

Monday

Tuesday

Wednesday

Thursday

Friday

Saturday

Sunday

Saturday and Sunday
are also called the **weekend.**

Many people
do not go to
school or work.

There are four weeks
in one **month**.

There are 12 months
in one **year**.

January	February	March
April	May	June
July	August	September
October	November	December

Everyone has a birthday, once a year, on the day they were born.

When is your birthday?

One year has 365 days.

A new year begins on
1 January.

There are many celebrations
all over the world.

Look!

The sun is in the sky.

It is morning again.

What will you
do today?

Glossary

hour an amount of time that is 60 minutes long

midnight in the middle of the night, when one day ends and another begins. Both hands of the clock are on twelve and it is dark outside.

month an amount of time. There are twelve months in one year.

second the time it takes to clap your hands once

week an amount of time that is seven days long

weekend the two days of the week that are also called Saturday and Sunday

year an amount of time that is twelve months long